2-D Shapes
Are Behind
the Drapes!

Tracy Kompelien

Consulting Editors, Diane Craig, M.A./Reading Specialist
and Susan Kosel, M.A. Education

ABDO
Publishing Company

Published by ABDO Publishing Company, 4940 Viking Drive, Edina, Minnesota 55435.

Printed in the United States.

Credits
Edited by: Pam Price
Curriculum Coordinator: Nancy Tuminelly
Cover and Interior Design and Production: Mighty Media
Photo Credits: AbleStock, ShutterStock, Wewerka Photography

Library of Congress Cataloging-in-Publication Data

Kompelien, Tracy, 1975-
    2-d shapes are behind the drapes! / Tracy Kompelien
      p. cm. -- (Math made fun)
    ISBN 10 1-59928-507-X (hardcover)
    ISBN 10 1-59928-508-8 (paperback)

    ISBN 13 978-1-59928-507-8 (hardcover)
    ISBN 13 978-1-59928-508-5 (paperback)
    1. Shapes--Juvenile literature. 2. Geometry--Juvenile literature. I. Title. II. Series.

    QA445.5.K658 2007
    516'.154--dc22

                                                                2006012570

SandCastle Level: Transitional

SandCastle™ books are created by a professional team of educators, reading specialists, and content developers around five essential components—phonemic awareness, phonics, vocabulary, text comprehension, and fluency—to assist young readers as they develop reading skills and strategies and increase their general knowledge. All books are written, reviewed, and leveled for guided reading, early reading intervention, and Accelerated Reader® programs for use in shared, guided, and independent reading and writing activities to support a balanced approach to literacy instruction. The SandCastle™ series has four levels that correspond to early literacy development. The levels help teachers and parents select appropriate books for young readers.

Emerging Readers   **Beginning Readers**   **Transitional Readers**   **Fluent Readers**
(no flags)   (1 flag)   (2 flags)   (3 flags)

These levels are meant only as a guide. All levels are subject to change.

A shape

is the form or outline
of an arrangement.

Words used to
describe shapes:

angle	round
circle	square
diamond	triangle
oval	2-D
rectangle	

This is a circle.

I know that this is a circle because it is round and the distance from the center to the outside is the same.

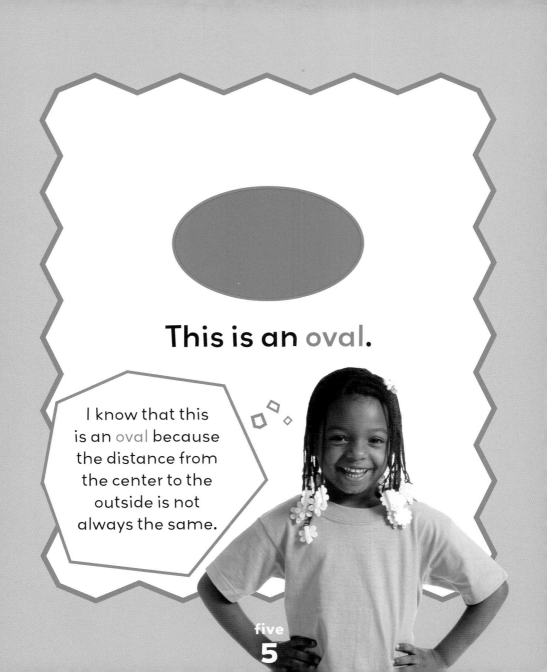

This is an oval.

I know that this is an oval because the distance from the center to the outside is not always the same.

This is a square**.**

A square has
four angles and
four sides that
are the same
length.

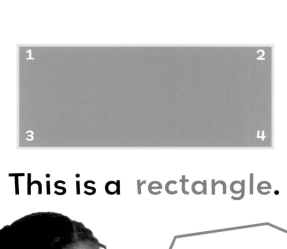

This is a rectangle.

A rectangle has four angles and four sides. The opposite sides are the same length.

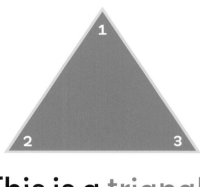

This is a triangle.

A triangle has three sides and three angles.

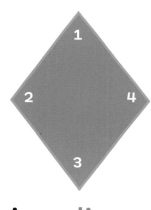

This is a diamond.

A diamond has four sides. Its angles form points at the top, bottom, and sides.

2-D Shapes Are behind the Drapes!

Shane sees 2-D shapes that are alike.

Shane sees two ⭕⭕ on his 🚲.

I know that the wheels on my bike are circles because all points on a circle are the same distance from the center.

twelve

12

Shane's room has

purple 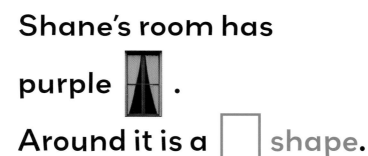 .

Around it is a ☐ shape.

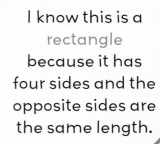

I know this is a
rectangle
because it has
four sides and the
opposite sides are
the same length.

Shane's mom makes a  for lunch. It's fun to have to munch!

I know that these are triangles. They each have three sides and three angles.

Seeing 2-D Shapes Every Day!

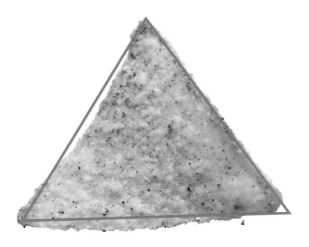

Sherry sees shapes everywhere, even at her birthday party. The chip is shaped like a triangle.

The chip has three sides and three angles. It is shaped like a triangle.

eighteen
18

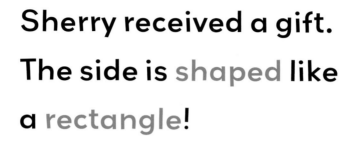

Sherry received a gift. The side is shaped like a rectangle!

I know that this shape has four sides and four angles. The opposite sides are the same length. This means it is a rectangle.

Happy Birthday

Sherry's birthday card is also shaped like a rectangle!

I know the card is a rectangle because it has four sides and four right angles.

How many shapes can you find in the picture?

Think about how many sides and angles the figures have. Shapes are around you every day!

Glossary

angle – the shape formed when two lines meet at a common point.

drape – a curtain.

equal – having exactly the same size or amount.

length – the distance from one end of an object to the other.

side – a line segment in a shape.

2-D – having length and width but no height, flat.